Accelerating Sustainability Using the 80/20 Rule

Gareth Kane

Terra Infirma Ltd

gareth@terrainfirma.co.uk

First published in 2014 by Dō Sustainability

87 Lonsdale Road, Oxford OX2 7ET, UK

ISBN 978-1-910174-39-5 (eBook-ePub)
ISBN 978-1-910174-40-1 (eBook-PDF)
ISBN 978-1-910174-38-8 (Paperback)

A catalogue record for this title is available from the British Library.

Dō Sustainability strives for net positive social and environmental impact. See our sustainability policy at **www.dosustainability.com**.

Page design and typesetting by Alison Rayner
Cover by Becky Chilcott

For further information on Dō Sustainability, visit our website:
www.dosustainability.com

DōShorts

Dō Sustainability is the publisher of DōShorts: short, high-value business guides that distil sustainability best practice and business insights for busy, results-driven professionals. Each DōShort can be read in 90 minutes.

New and forthcoming DōShorts – stay up to date

We publish new DōShorts each month. The best way to keep up to date? Sign up to our short, monthly newsletter. Go to **www.dosustainability. com/newsletter** to sign up to the Dō Newsletter. Some of our latest and forthcoming titles include:

- *Understanding Integrated Reporting: The Concise Guide to Integrated Thinking and the Future of Corporate Reporting* Carol Adams

- *Corporate Sustainability in India: A Practical Guide for Multinationals* Caroline Twigg

- *Networks for Sustainability: Harnessing People Power to Deliver Your Goals* Sarah Holloway

- *Making Sustainability Matter: How To Make Materiality Drive Profit, Strategy and Communications* Dwayne Baraka

- *Creating a Sustainable Brand: A Guide to Growing the Sustainability Top Line* Henk Campher

- *Cultivating System Change: A Practitioner's Companion* Anna Birney

- *How Much Energy Does Your Building Use?* Liz Reason

- *Lobbying for Good: How Business Advocacy Can Accelerate the Delivery of a Sustainable Economy* Paul Monaghan & Philip Monaghan

- *Creating Employee Champions: How to Drive Business Success Through Sustainability Engagement Training*   Joanna M. Sullivan
- *Smart Engagement: Why, What, Who and How*   John Aston & Alan Knight
- *How to Produce a Sustainability Report*   Kye Gbangbola & Nicole Lawler
- *Strategic Sustainable Procurement: An Overview of Law and Best Practice for the Public and Private Sectors*   Colleen Theron & Malcolm Dowden
- *The Reputation Risk Handbook: Surviving and Thriving in the Age of Hyper-Transparency*   Andrea Bonime-Blanc
- *Business Strategy for Water Challenges: From Risk to Opportunity*   Stuart Orr and Guy Pegram

Subscriptions

In addition to individual sales of our ebooks, we now offer subscriptions. Access 60+ ebooks for the price of 6 with a personal subscription to our full e-library. Institutional subscriptions are also available for your staff or students. Visit **www.dosustainability.com/books/subscriptions** or email **veruschka@dosustainability.com**

Write for us, or suggest a DōShort

Please visit **www.dosustainability.com** for our full publishing programme. If you don't find what you need, write for us! Or suggest a DōShort on our website. We look forward to hearing from you.

Abstract

WE ARE NOW RECEIVING clear signals that our collective way of life is rubbing up against the natural limits of the planet. We need to tackle climate change, resource depletion, loss of biodiversity and the build-up of persistent toxic chemicals in the environment, and it is imperative that we act decisively and quickly. Unfortunately, most organisations' attempts to address these huge, existential challenges are often bogged down in a mire of bureaucracy, obsession with detail and eco-waffle, leading to incremental improvements at best. It does not take a genius to see that it is time to scrape the mud off our boots and find a short, fast path towards sustainability. Fortunately a natural rule of statistics – the Power Law – can come to our aid. The Law says that, in many situations, a small number of input variables determines the vast majority of the results. This is commonly known as the 80/20 Rule, as 80 percent of outputs are typically produced by 20 percent of inputs. It follows that if we identify these 'vital few' inputs in sustainability and focus our efforts on them, we can maximise our effectiveness and accelerate progress rapidly. This book develops that theme to help you start thinking about sustainability from an 80/20 perspective. So, if you want to pull yourself free from the mire in which many sustainability practitioners get stuck, focus on what matters, and start making a real difference, then this book is for you!

About the Author

 **GARETH KANE** has spent the last 16 years trying to bring some common sense to the sustainability debate. His consultancy, Terra Infirma Ltd, has attracted a long list of blue-chip clients such as the BBC, BAE Systems plc, Johnson Matthey plc, Viridor, News International (now News UK) and the NHS. He runs the Corporate Sustainability Mastermind Group – a small gathering of top sustainability executives, which meets quarterly to discuss sustainability issues and share best practice.

Gareth has previously authored four books: *The Three Secrets of Green Business, The Green Executive: Corporate Leadership for a Low Carbon Economy, Green Jujitsu: The Smart Way to Engage Employees in Sustainability* and *Building a Sustainable Supply Chain*. He also presents the popular 'Ask Gareth' sustainability series on YouTube.

Acknowledgments

FIRST OF ALL, I must thank all those who contributed their time and expertise in the form of interviews conducted over the last four years which form the basis of many case studies in this book: Paul Taylor, Sustainability Manager at Camira Fabrics, Tracy Rawling Church, Head of CSR at Kyocera Document Solutions UK, Tom Smith, Head of Marketing and Business Development at Sedex, Sean Axon, Group Sustainability Director at Johnson Matthey plc, Ramon Arratia, Sustainability Director at Interface EMEAI, Roberta Barbieri of Diageo and Glen Bennett of EAE Ltd.

Thanks must also go to my consultancy clients and Corporate Sustainability Mastermind Group members for sharing insights; the latter contributions must remain anonymous under group rules.

Second, I'd like to thank the team at Dō Sustainability for commissioning this book, in particular, Rob West who had the original idea for a Dō Short on the 80/20 Rule and then found I had blogged in the topic! And of course Nick Bellorini and Gudrun Freece who will no doubt have had a hand in you getting to hear about it.

And last but not least, I'd like to thank my family: Karen and the Kane boys, Harry, Jimmy and Charlie, for keeping me sane and reminding me why I'm doing this – to create a better future for the next generation.

Contents

CHAPTER 1
Introduction

THERE IS A BRILLIANT Dilbert cartoon strip where Dilbert tells his boss: 'We replaced our styrofoam coffee cups with paper cups. But it's not so clear it helps the planet.' 'We didn't do it to help the planet,' retorts pointy-haired boss. 'We did it to look like the sort of company that cares about that sort of thing.' Leaving the cynicism aside, the cartoon neatly parodies the tendency of sustainability professionals to focus their energies on making changes with negligible practical impact.

Sustainability is undoubtedly the single biggest challenge for the human race. Climate change, resource depletion, biodiversity loss and the build-up of persistent toxic chemicals show that we are rubbing up against the natural limits of the planet. Arguing over the right kind of coffee cup in the light of these existential threats makes fiddling while Rome burns look like a proactive game-changer by comparison.

A different threat to tackling climate change and other global challenges is green self-indulgence. Doug Tompkins, founder of North Face and Esprit recently told Guardian Sustainable Business:

> *We should not rush into trying to solve problems before we have truly understood the deep dynamics of the system we are seeking to transform . . . what we need is idea work, which helps build the intellectual infrastructure necessary to make deep structural changes in the economic technologies that we use to operate our*

societies. For ultimately, there can be no hope of ending the eco-social crisis until people abandon the arrogance of humanism and adopt an eco-centric worldview.[1]

This kind of eco-waffle drives me up the wall. The climate does not care whether a kilo of carbon dioxide has been emitted while listening to whale music or watching *The X Factor*. It is a kilo of carbon molecules which causes a certain amount of global warming. We need to cut carbon, not achieve enlightenment. If we get more spiritually enlightened by doing so, then great, but let's put the horse in front of the cart where it belongs.

Second, the science tells us we should act swiftly. Given the residence time of carbon in the atmosphere, and the presence of worrying tipping points in the climate system, cutting a kilo of carbon now is much more beneficial than cutting a kilo of carbon next year. Sitting in a yurt chanting or stroking our beards in the wilderness may be self-fulfilling, but it must not be confused for practical progress. We must learn by doing, be prepared to make mistakes, but it is paramount we get going.

One positive feature of the last 10 years has been the rise of what I call The Pragmatic Environmentalist. This can-do breed is free from the ideological baggage of the traditional tree-hugger. They will embrace any technology, market mechanism or technique if it will contribute to sustainability. With their championing of nuclear energy and genetic technology in particular, they can seem heretical to the hippie brigade, but if a genetically modified algae can create biodiesel out of atmospheric carbon dioxide, why would we write it off?

One of the features of these new environmentalists is their background. While some have emerged from mainstream environmentalism but have grown tired of 'paralysis by perfectionism', others come from engineering and even military backgrounds. These people love to be given a problem to solve and will set about that problem with gusto – without worrying about an eco-centric worldview. They just get on with it.

This book is a clarion call for all sustainability professionals to focus on what matters. It takes as its basis the 80/20 Rule, or Pareto Principle, which says that in many cases 20 percent of effort delivers 80 percent of results and, conversely, 80 percent of effort only manages to deliver 20 percent. By identifying and focusing on the 'good' 20 percent and stripping out the ineffective 80 percent, we can rapidly accelerate progress towards our ultimate goal of sustainability. The brutality of the 80/20 Rule can unsettle the more timid of the green-minded, but it is a key weapon of the pragmatic environmentalist.

....

CHAPTER 2

What is the Pareto Principle?

The 80/20 Rule – From peas to the Power Law

VILFREDO PARETO (1848–1923) was an Italian economist who noticed the tendency for many completely different things to be distributed very unevenly, but unevenly in a *predictable* way. He was studying wealth distribution in thirteenth-century England when he found that roughly 20 percent of the population owned 80 percent of the wealth. This correlated with his observation that 80 percent of the peas from his garden were found in 20 percent of pods and he noticed that this rule of thumb applied many other unrelated natural phenomena. Unfortunately, Pareto's work and social beliefs have been conflated with fascism, rightly or wrongly, and he fell out of favour in the first half of the twentieth century.[2]

Pareto never mentioned the 80/20 Rule or named it after himself. It was management consultant Joseph Juran who dusted off the theory in the 1950s, named it 'The Pareto Principle' and started applying it to business.[3] He initially described it as 'the vital few and the trivial many', but later changed this to 'the vital few and the useful many' to acknowledge the remaining 80 percent of the causes should not be totally ignored (an issue we will consider later in the chapter).

One of the earliest applications of the 80/20 Rule was in computing. IBM realised that 80 percent of processing time was spent on 20 percent of processes. They focused their efforts on making those processes more efficient which led to huge leaps forward in processor speed. Later Microsoft found that by targeting the 20 percent most reported problems, they could solve 80 percent of system crashes.[4]

The 80/20 Rule can be seen in many different arenas. In my consultancy business, Terra Infirma Ltd, 20 percent of our clients represent 79.1 percent of our income. On the Terra Infirma YouTube channel, 81 percent of views arise from 19 percent of the uploaded videos.

The mathematical basis for the 80/20 Rule is the Power Law distribution (see Figure 1). This is clearly different to the better-known 'normal distribution' where data are distributed around the average in a neat bell curve – which you would get if you measured, say, the heights of adults.

FIGURE 1. Power Law and normal distributions.

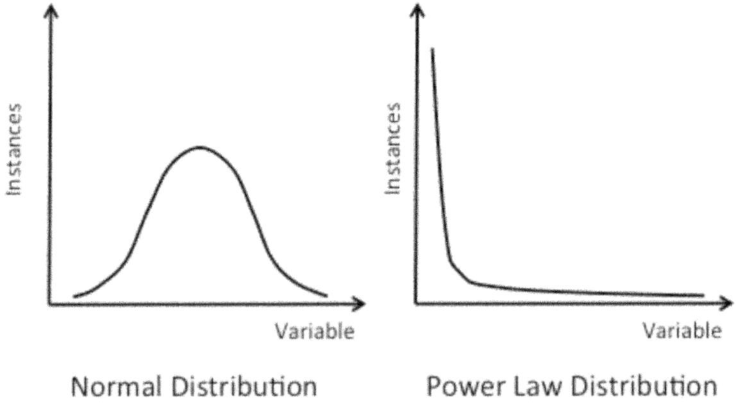

Normal Distribution   Power Law Distribution

One of the foremost promoters of the 80/20 Rule in business and life is Richard Koch, author of the book *The 80/20 Principle*.[5] Koch proposes using the principle in two subtly different ways:

- 80/20 analysis where you use empirical evidence to identify the 20 percent of issues which deliver 80 percent of results;

- 80/20 thinking where you take a much more intuitive approach to identifying the 20 percent.

More recently, 'life hacking' guru Tim Ferriss has popularised the use of the 80/20 idea to set out a philosophy of getting maximum results from the least possible effort through best-selling books such as *The Four Hour Work Week.*[6]

Implications of the 80/20 Rule

The basic idea of the 80/20 Rule is that you will be much more effective if you put your energy into the 20 percent of activities that deliver 80 percent of the results and put less emphasis the 80 percent which deliver only 20 percent. Conversely you may want to consider why the 80 percent of your efforts deliver so little and remove the constraints.

It is important not to get too hung up on the numbers 80 and 20. Whether the distribution is 90/10 or 70/30, the same principle applies: much of life is predictably unequal. In this book I am not intending to prove the 80/20 Rule, or that it applies to sustainability, although we will be looking at some examples below. Rather, my intention is to provide 80/20 tools which will help you clear away the clutter from your to-do list and focus on the techniques which deliver great results. As Koch notes, you can either be analytical with the rule, or use it as a general guide. We will be doing both in this book.

Examples from sustainability

There are numerous examples of 80/20-style imbalances in the sustainability sphere. Probably the most pronounced is in the distribution of wealth where the richest 1 percent of people own 54 percent of the wealth. Depending on how you assess income, 20 percent of the population earn between 70 and 83 percent of global income with just 1 percent going to the bottom 20 percent.[7]

Looking at environmental impacts, in 1998, 20 percent of the world's population consumed 68 percent of energy,[8] although this imbalance had reduced by 2010 when 33 percent of people consumed 66 percent of the total.[9] In the UK, the richest 10 percent produce twice the carbon emissions as the poorest 10 percent. In Sweden it's four times as much, in China it's 18 times as much.[10]

Toyota released a study of the life cycle carbon emissions of a typical car which showed that 20 percent of the footprint came from its manufacture and 80 percent from its use, although this appears to be falling as fuel efficiency improves.[11] Likewise the BBC found that 20 percent of the footprint of a television programme came from production (cameras, lights, computers, logistics, etc.) and 80 percent from consumption (all those widescreen TVs and set-top boxes).[12] Proctor & Gamble found that 75 percent of the energy use over the life cycle of washing powder was down to a single factor – heating water to wash the clothes.[13]

All of these examples illustrate that the really significant sustainability issues in many product/service sectors are often determined by a very small number of factors. Therefore it is clear that the 80/20 Rule has many applications in sustainability and we can use it to accelerate progress.

Limitations of the 80/20 Rule

It is very telling that Juran changed his view of 80/20 from 'the vital few and the trivial many' to 'the vital few and the useful many'. Here are some examples where 'the useful many' can be important in sustainability:

- Engaging people: as Sean Axon, Global Sustainability Director of Johnson Matthey plc puts it: 'although the 20% [the vital issues] is what makes all the difference, the 80% often is the way to engage employees by getting them involved in issues which they are familiar with'.

- Issues of popular concern: all too often the public/media perception of environmental issues is at odds with the objective evidence – for example, the calls to tax single-use plastic bags. However, if you are seen to be neglecting such simple but symbolic issues, it can undermine trust in your claims to be tackling the big issues and making a real difference.

- Kaizen-style continual improvement gains: the cumulative impact of lots of small incremental improvements can in many cases add up to significant gains. A modern car's internal combustion engine is fundamentally the same as that in a Ford Model T, yet many thousands of incremental improvements in technology have made the modern version several times more efficient.

My model of change towards sustainability is the 'sloping staircase' – a series of step changes interspaced with periods of continual improvement (see Figure 2). The step changes result from the vital 20 percent of actions which make a real difference, while the incremental improvements keep squeezing more out of the system at each stage. However, the general pattern is that too many people focus on the 80 percent and shy away from the vital 20 percent – and end up on the diminishing returns trajectory as a result.

....

FIGURE 2. The sloping staircase model of change.

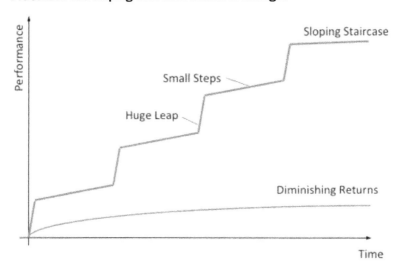

While the main message of this book is how to do sustainability properly by applying 80/20 thinking, it is not carved in stone. The 20 percent will make the difference. A minority of the 80 percent of potential sustainability actions are important in their own way, but many, if not most, are a waste of time and energy.

Risks in using the 80/20 Rule

As well as the limitations above, there are a number of risks in using the rule in an over-simplistic way:

- Applying the rule to the wrong variable. Koch uses the example of a bookshop. If you apply the 80/20 Rule to the books and get rid of 80 percent of the stock, you may put off customers who want to browse, even if they end up buying a bestseller. He recommends focusing on the desires of the 20 percent of customers who provide 80 percent of sales instead.

- Not considering the time factor: in the bookshop example, a bestseller may provide the bulk of sales in a single year before fading quickly, but a more prosaic title may sell more copies over 10 or 20 years.

So while we will be looking at how we can apply the 80/20 Rule to accelerate sustainability, it is imperative that the principle is applied carefully.

....

CHAPTER 3

Using the 80/20 Rule to Deliver More Quick Wins More Quickly

Overview

IT MAY BE SURPRISING to start a book on the 80/20 Rule to describe its application to identifying quick wins as these are usually in the 80 percent of minor issues. However, an 80/20 mindset can help you identify and tackle those opportunities where a small change can have a disproportionate benefit in a very short timeframe. This is particularly important where resources are very limited and/or if you want to demonstrate the financial benefits of sustainability to a sceptical audience.

In this section we will look at how to use 80/20 thinking to identify the most effective solutions in waste minimisation, energy efficiency, water conservation and transport.

Waste minimisation

In manufacturing, the most expensive and environmentally damaging place to create waste is at the end of the production process. I once followed through the production line at a cutting-edge pharmaceutical plant – all clean rooms, hi-technology and 'space suits' – to the packing line. Here, where the value added to the raw materials was at its maximum value, the packaging machine was malfunctioning so badly that employees were literally shovelling heaps of pills off the floor and into the bin. They might as well have been shovelling money into a furnace.

Likewise, I followed through the production process for bespoke kitchen units only to find a whole stack of completed kits which had been set aside because forklift truck drivers had damaged them. I saw exactly the same thing at the goods out area of a contract lubricant manufacturer where perfectly good products were waiting in unsalable dented cans – and clogging up the limited space available.

In all three cases the economic value and environmental impact em- bedded into the product was at its maximum when it was wasted. Therefore focusing attention at this end of the process will reap the biggest rewards. Getting packing machines properly set up, goods-out areas properly laid out and forklift drivers properly trained/incentivised will deliver significant results.

Other simple efforts which I have seen deliver substantial results include:

- Colour coding segregated waste bins consistently across the organisation (using standard colours where they exist, e.g. in the construction industry).

- Ensuring raw materials/components are purchased to the correct size and quantity.

- Ensuring machines are set up, calibrated and maintained properly to minimise off-spec product.

Energy efficiency

Energy bills can often be slashed with ease, if you focus on the actions that will make a difference. A careful analysis of consumption patterns, along with some experience and common sense, can flag up where your efforts will have maximum impact.

Compressed air is the most expensive and carbon-intensive form of energy in the average factory – as it takes an expensive form of energy (electricity) and inefficiently turns it into a form which is difficult to contain. Yet most people seem to treat it as if it was free – when I visit factories, I frequently find air lines leaking like sieves, air pressure too high, and redundant 'historic' air lines leading nowhere. The worst example I came across was a compressor shoved under a low roof with no cold air intake – it was breathing in its own exhaust and overheating so much that someone had put a huge industrial fan beside it to cool it down – wasting even more energy. In this case, the solution was as simple as drilling a hole in the wall and connecting the air intake to the outside world with a short piece of hose.

LED lighting represents another brilliant quick win, reducing energy use by a factor of six in some trials.[14] Yes, it requires investment, but the return on investment is swift (one to two years in many cases) and the carbon reductions are quite remarkable. Automation of processes can help too, from sophisticated building management systems through 'Nightwatchman'-style software to switch off computers in the evening to simple PIR indicators to switch lights on and off when people are present.

Water conservation

Once you factor in purchase and treatment costs, water bills can rival energy bills. As leaks tend to lose water 24 hours a day, seven days a week, they should be hunted down and eliminated with extreme prejudice. Checking water consumption during downtime will give you an idea of the scale of the problem. An ultrasonic detector can help identify leaks in awkward places such as underground.

Other solutions are highly sector specific. For example, in flooring tile giant and sustainability pioneer InterfaceFLOR, adding a $10 nozzle to a particular part of the process led to $10,000 p.a. saving in water costs.[15]

Transport

In transportation, some very simple measures can lead to significant results. For example, a major public sector organisation I worked with reduced their fuel bill by 20 percent overnight by fitting trackers to the fleet. This cut out unauthorised use of the vehicles and increased the performance of the departments concerned to boot.

In many cases, the key to unlocking transport improvements is to remove barriers to using the greener option. For example, in a workshop I was running at a major international client, someone complained that no-one was using the company's teleconferencing system. We discovered that in order to calculate the financial benefits of the system, the company made it a condition of booking that an estimation of avoided staff travel time and travel costs had to be provided. So if you wanted to use the system, you'd have to sit down and work out where everyone was coming from, how they were travelling, how long it would take them, what each person's hourly cost was and what fares/hire car charges/mileage they would incur. If you wanted to hold a usual meeting, you'd simply schedule it on everybody's calendar and book a meeting room, so people were sticking with the traditional system. When we stripped out the measurement system, the company had to invest to double the capacity of the teleconferencing as it became so popular.

Summary

Quick wins will not deliver sustainability on their own, but applying the 80/20 Rule can ensure that the effort put into resolving these issues delivers maximum outcomes. Some general principles are:

- Use cost as a simple indicator to identify the issues to address (e.g. damaged product, compressed air).

- Cut out the tinkering and address the issues where low-cost technology can deliver step changes in performance.

- Ask employees at the sharp end for ideas on how to improve the system (we will investigate this further in the next section).

- Eliminate barriers to green behaviour with extreme prejudice.

CHAPTER 4

Using the 80/20 Rule to Make Employee Engagement Effective

A 2014 STUDY of more than 700 companies by the 2degrees network found that the two biggest challenges facing sustainability practitioners are:

- Engaging the boardroom in sustainability.

- Engaging everybody else in sustainability.[16]

The need for such engagement is critical – step changes will not happen without buy-in from the board, and no change will be effective unless employees in general come on board. You can purchase all the shiny technology you want, but if people aren't aware, willing and able to use it, it will simply gather dust. Therefore employee engagement is most definitely a 'vital 20 percent issue'.

Unfortunately, as we will see below, a significant proportion of 'standard practice' is completely ineffective. Even more unfortunate is that this fact doesn't dissuade practitioners from trying the same old thing over and over again – classic 80 percent behaviour.

There are two angles to using the 80/20 Rule in employee engagement that we will consider in this chapter:

- What works: stripping out the 80 percent of ineffective engagement activity and focusing on the 20 percent of elements which deliver significant results.

- 80/20 mentality: creating a culture where step changes are prized and 'box-ticking' is seen as a bad thing.

Why your employee engagement doesn't work

I fell into employee engagement by accident – I'm an engineer, not an occupational psychologist – but my client base started asking me whether I could help them tackle this vital issue. My engineering instinct soon told me that most efforts at employee engagement were completely ineffective, yet were earnestly replicated in organisation after organisation despite any evidence of positive results.

The standard techniques include:

- 'Switch it off' stickers on light switches.

- Posters urging people to consider the environment.

- Hand-outs of jute bags containing energy efficient light bulbs and FairTrade chocolate.

- Putting chocolates on the keyboards of employees who switch their computers off overnight.

- Networks of green champions.

In practice, I frequently walk into rooms with a 'switch it off' sticker where the lights are blazing and all the computers are left on. Gimmicks soon get forgotten or lose their impact. And I have never met a happy network of green champions – the champions I speak to are usually left disillusioned by their inability to make change happen.

So why don't these approaches work?

- The injunctions to act get lost among the noise of the multitude of messages we are bombarded with every day.

- People generally resent being hectored and may resist as a reflex reaction.

- There's no explanation of the benefits of this action either to the individual, the business or wider society.

- Familiarity breeds contempt – you soon stop noticing the signs and posters.

- The message is usually uninspiring, lifeless and dull.

Green Jujitsu

So, given the fact that the 'standard' engagement techniques don't work, what is left? Well, I found through trial and error that the most effective approaches to engaging employees in sustainability involved aligning the approach to the prevailing culture in the organisation (or a particular department in that organisation), rather than trying to change the culture wholesale.

My initial successes were in engineering companies where I felt comfortable with the culture. Instead of trying to convert engineers into tree-huggers over the course of an hour-long engagement session, I reframed sustainability in the organisation as an engineering problem requiring technical and behavioural solutions. Engineers love solving problems, so they rolled up their sleeves and got stuck in (we'll look in more detail at the techniques below). Following initial successes, we started looking at how human interest stories involving engineers solving such problems could be used to inspire others and the approach snowballed from there.

In another case, I helped a major media group develop a new approach to employee engagement based on the culture of journalism. In particular, the company is now using punchy headlines, human-interest stories and infographics – all standard journalistic tools – to communicate sustainability issues in a format which will appeal to its employees. This in turn is translating into action on the ground.

I call this approach 'Green Jujitsu'.[17] A jujitsu expert sees their opponent's strengths, weight, height and momentum as opportunities to win their bout – unlike boxing where you focus on battering the opponent into submission. In Green Jujitsu we focus on people's strengths, habits and interests rather than trying to correct perceived weaknesses.

Effective engagement techniques

In my experience, the most powerful Green Jujitsu technique is the solutions workshop. The basic idea is simple: you get employees in a room, divide them into teams and get them to come up with ideas on how to improve environmental performance in their immediate work environment. The benefits of this approach are:

- Employees get a much more fundamental understanding of issues as it applies to their sphere of influence at work.

- You get instant buy-in as the employees now have 'skin in the game' when it comes to implementing changes.

- The practical, team-based approach makes it much harder for disinterested employees to switch off.

- You end up with dozens if not hundreds of practical ideas for changes which you can filter to find the 80/20-style quick wins we looked at the last chapter.

The workshop itself can be designed to resonate with the culture of attendees. For engineers I use a fishbone diagram – an engineering tool – as a template. For non-technical staff, I tend to use a simple mindmap, which is less threatening to many people.

Another simple but powerful Green Jujitsu technique is the question. Questions are disarming, rather than threatening, and put the emphasis on the audience to think through the answer. For example, instead of trying to persuade senior employees why they should take sustainability seriously, my standard approach is to ask them why they should (see below).

Focused engagement

While I was writing this book, I had a meeting with representatives of a large construction company about employee engagement. They told me their challenge was how to engage with their large number of front-line workers. These people were often on either short-term contracts or employed via subcontractors, so there was a constant churn in individuals, and very few, if any, had access to IT systems. We mulled on this for a while, before I asked how much of an environmental problem it was. 'Oh, about 10% of our impact relates to on-site activity, 90% is locked in at the design stage.' Given that 80/20 was at the top of my mind, I asked them: 'Why struggle to engage the large number of hard-to-reach front-line workers with little influence, when the relatively small number of people who determine 90% of the impact are very easy to reach?' They readily agreed, and the relief was palpable. This is a classic case of how 80/20 thinking shifted our focus from 'what's the most difficult challenge?' to 'what's the most significant challenge?'

Ramon Arratia at Interface is very focused on engaging people who have influence on sustainability in the business:

> *We tell our employees about Mission Zero and what they have to do, but we only engage intensively with employees who carry influence on sustainability. Engagement for the sake of it doesn't have any value.*

> *So we identify the people with biggest influence on Mission Zero and try to enable them to use that influence in a positive way – 'Can you give me a product which has zero CO_2?' or 'Can you give me this raw material in a recycled form?' We give them budget, time and exposure to get on with it.*

Aligning responsibility to authority

As we have seen, one key 80/20 Rule is to focus engagement on those with influence on sustainability. But unfortunately in most organisations there is a fundamental structural problem – a mismatch between those with strong influence over sustainability issues and the delegation of responsibility.

Most environmental managers have a huge amount of responsibility, including keeping their bosses out of jail, but precious little authority to act outside a very narrow silo. How do we expect people to make change with both hands tied behind their backs?

The epitome of this mismatch is the widespread use of so-called green champions to deliver sustainability. Why this approach is so popular when it transfers responsibility for change onto people with absolutely no authority to act, I will never understand. The majority of green champions networks I encounter are, unsurprisingly, dysfunctional.

The only way to do sustainability properly is a proper allocation of responsibility to those with authority. So production managers, site managers, procurement managers, energy managers, product developers, business developers, marketing and public relations people – everyone with influence – should have appropriate sustainability objectives and targets hardwired into their job descriptions.

Getting the board on board for sustainability

In my book *The Green Executive*[18] I make the case that the difference between the best and the rest in sustainability is leadership. The one thing that links the companies leading the way on sustainability is a tangible commitment from the very top. It was the late Ray Anderson of Interface who launched Mission Zero, Sir Stuart Rose of Marks & Spencer put £200 million into the retailer's Plan A sustainability programme before there was a plan, and Paul Polman is driving Unilever's sustainability programme forward – all chief executives leading the way. Without such leadership, major investments for sustainability will not be made, strategic decisions will not factor in sustainability issues and employees will become disillusioned. Therefore leadership is clearly a 'vital 20 percent' issue.

However, as the 2degrees survey mentioned above indicated, engaging the board is a very real challenge. Green Jujitsu gives us the following tactics to help:

- Choose language very carefully. Translate your sustainability programme into the language your board uses such as 'competitive advantage', 'strategic risk' and 'return on investment'.

- Make sure you reframe any conversation away from the standard 'profit or sustainability' mindset and towards 'profit through sustainability'. Likewise you need to communicate the risks of 'do nothing'.

- Challenge board members to work through the business case themselves. Board members generally don't like to be told they don't understand something, so it is better to get them to explore it for themselves.

- Identify which competitors are performing sustainability better and use them as a comparator. Senior executives tend to be very competitive and this can be a powerful spur.

- Engineer an opportunity to get a particular board member to speak publicly on sustainability. The background reading Interface's Ray Anderson had to undertake for such a speech was the spark for Mission Zero.[19]

Getting people to think 80/20

Of course, if we are going to adopt the 80/20 Rule, then we need to get the employees not just thinking of sustainability, but '80/20 sustainability'.

As Paul Taylor of Camira says:

The approach [at Camira] has been 'go big' – it comes back to the culture because the culture here is 'there's no need to do all this tinkering around the edges'. We get it and everybody who comes into the business gets it, because it is part of the interview process.

The 'go big' mentality is essential, both to tackle problems properly, but also to make the engagement authentic. All too often there is a mismatch between the scale of the threat of, say, climate change and the ambition of solutions suggested to meet that threat. A great example would be the Live8 concert in 2005 that told us that we should tackle the existential threat of climate change by not leaving our phone chargers plugged in overnight or re-using our shopping bags. People are not stupid and they will recognise that it will take more than these tweaks even to start solving the problem – and they'll lose faith in the engagement as a result.

So how do we instil the 80/20 thinking in our colleagues? Here are a number of key factors which will help:

- Strong pronouncements and corresponding actions from those in leadership positions (people believe what they see, not what they hear).

- Setting stretch targets on sustainability: we will be covering this in more detail in Chapter 8.

- Embedding those stretch targets into the reporting structure to force people to face up to the scale of the challenge.

- Encouraging a 'learn by doing' culture which encourages lateral thinking.

- Developing training sessions which demonstrate the opportunities presented by 80/20 thinking in areas such as product design and procurement.

- Use of inspiring case studies which deliver 80/20 type results.

- Providing sufficient resources to enable change.

Summary

We have seen how engaging employees is seen as one of the key sustainability challenges. Unfortunately most efforts are mired in the 80 percent of activities which will deliver marginal improvements at best. Green Jujitsu is an attempt to turn this on its head and make sustainability relevant to employees, particularly those in key positions of influence. The biggest priority should be engaging those with most influence – the organisation's leadership.

It is essential also that we make the aim of the engagement to distil 80/20 thinking in others. This will help drive 80/20 style changes and make the engagement more authentic and effective as a result.
....

CHAPTER 5

Using the 80/20 Rule in Indicators and Quantitative Analysis

Overview

'IF YOU CAN'T MEASURE IT, you can't manage it', the old management adage goes. But sustainability measures such as life cycle assessments and carbon footprints are incredibly data-intensive – and thus time-consuming and expensive – and can be highly dependent on a small number of assumptions. This can lead to 'paralysis by analysis' where the process of measuring becomes an end in itself and stops you actually doing anything practical based on the data. 'A pig never got fat by weighing it' is the counter-balancing old farmers' saying to those obsessed with data.

So what can you do to short cut the measurement process? This chapter looks at the methods you can use to measure what matters and avoid getting bogged down in the minor detail.

Materiality and significance

Most global environmental standards such as the Global Reporting Initiative (GRI) Guidelines and ISO14001 contain mechanisms to filter out insignificant and irrelevant issues.

The GRI says the following about materiality in its G4 guidelines:[20]

G4 has an increased emphasis on the need for organizations to focus the reporting process and final report on those topics that are material to their business and their key stakeholders . . . While organizations may monitor and manage a far wider array of sustainability-related topics due to their everyday management activities, this new focus on materiality means that sustainability reports will be centred on matters that are really critical in order to achieve the organization's goals and manage its impact on society.

The G4 standard goes on to define 'material aspects' as:

Material aspects are those that reflect the organization's significant economic, environmental and social impacts; or substantively influence the assessments and decisions of stakeholders.

It is interesting that the standard allows for inequality of importance among material aspects:

Materiality is the threshold at which Aspects become sufficiently important that they should be reported. Beyond this threshold, not all material Aspects are of equal importance and the emphasis within a report should reflect the relative priority of these material Aspects.

But it is left to the organisation to define how the threshold of 'materiality' is defined:

A combination of internal and external factors should be used to determine whether an Aspect is material, including factors such as the organization's overall mission and competitive strategy, concerns expressed directly by stakeholders, broader social expectations, and the organization's influence on upstream (such as supply chain) and downstream (such as customers) entities.

ISO 14001 has a simpler definition of significant aspects:

A significant environmental aspect is an environmental aspect that has or can have a significant environmental impact.

Again, it is left to the organisation to define the method of assessing significant impact and to set the threshold within that method.

While an element of focusing on the most important issues is embedded in these two standards, it is unlikely that they will allow you focus your efforts down as narrowly as required by 80/20 thinking. I recommend two tiers of indicators – a broader set material/significant issues and a subset representing priority issues (such as those in your strategy – see Chapter 8). The advantages of this approach are:

- You won't fall foul of third party accreditors, yet still retain your 80/20 priorities.

- The broader set will act as a warning system in case your attempts to focus on the big issues shift problems around rather than tackling them head on (for example, if an attempt to save water led to the introduction of noxious chemicals).

Iterative assessments

Life Cycle Assessment (LCA) is the process of assessing the environmental impacts of a product from cradle (raw material extraction) to grave (eventual disposal). The material and energy flows at each life cycle stage are collected together into an inventory, translated into a number of environmental impacts (global warming potential, acidification, etc.) and then translated into one or more indicators. While some form of LCA is essential part of eco-design process, there are a huge number of drawbacks:

- The process is highly data-intensive and therefore costly (an electronics firm told me over a decade ago that they budget £10,000 per component for a LCA of their products).

- The result can hinge on a small number of very uncertain life cycle variables (for example, a mobile phone may last until it wears out, replaced when lost or stolen, or it may be discarded when a new, more fashionable model is released).

- The mashing together of a range of environmental impacts into a single indicator (or a small number of indicators) has a mathematical tendency to bring issues to the same level.

An iterative life cycle assessment can help sort what matters from what does not. An outline of the process would be:

- List the different components of the product.

- Group these in terms of environmental importance either using judgement or a simple screening indicator such as cost, energy or mass of material.

- Collect detailed data for first group of components and carry out the life cycle assessment.

- Add the second group in and check the effect on the results.

- Repeat until adding further groups makes a negligible change, then stop.

The ISO14040 standard makes reference to LCA being an iterative process, but normally LCAs don't go to the lengths described above.

Data quality management

The main challenge in completing a life cycle assessment or a carbon footprint is gathering reliable data. It is particularly difficult to secure data from the supply chain, especially from primary industries where the impacts are greatest, but the reliability and accessibility of data is lowest. Commercial databases of generic life cycle information are available, giving, for example, the life cycle impacts of the average tonne of concrete or kilowatt of electricity, but these averages could obscure a very large or small impact in the particular case under study.

The 80/20 Rule can help with this problem. As mentioned above, the results of a life cycle assessment usually hinge on a small number of variables. Therefore if you identify these key variables and focus your resources on getting the best quality data for them, you can use generic data for the 80% of variables with minimal influence if high quality data aren't readily available. This will slash the time and effort required to collect data down to the bone.

A simple data quality management system can help you ensure you get the most accurate data where it counts. For example, in my MPhil studies my life cycle assessment model allowed the user to designate the quality of each piece of input data as 'high' (taken from real life), 'medium' (generic data which should be broadly representative of this case) or 'low' (an informed guess). The model would automatically test which pieces of data had the greatest effect on the results and flag up highly influential data which were designated 'low' or 'medium'. The user could then focus on getting the best data where it is needed rather than chasing precision where it wasn't important.

This method is not limited to life cycle assessment – exactly the same approach can be applied to carbon footprinting, ecological footprinting or any other data-intensive assessment process. It is fully compatible with the iterative assessment approach described above, improving the quality of the vital 20 percent of data inputs at each iteration.

Summary

In summary, it is important to apply 80/20 thinking to data collection and indicators to avoid 'paralysis by analysis'. By prioritising the really significant environmental issues, using iterative assessments and cleverly managing the quality of data collected, your analyses can give you or your stakeholders enough information to make decisions without getting bogged down in detail.

CHAPTER 6

Using the 80/20 Rule – Supply Chain

FOR MOST ORGANISATIONS, the environmental impact of their supply chain far outweighs that occurring within the factory fence/office walls. For example, carbon footprinting used to focus on on-site carbon emissions (commonly known as Scope 1) and those associated with electricity use on site (Scope 2). As Figure 3 demonstrates, supply chain emissions (Scope 3) tend to outstrip the others in significance and cannot be ignored.

....

FIGURE 3. Cradle to gate emissions for four major organisations.[21]

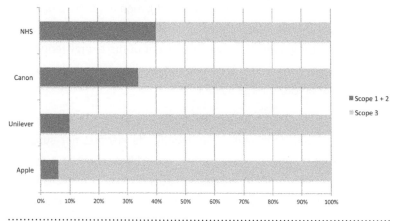

But the above analysis only covers issues we know, not the risks. Most of the big corporate environmental scandals of recent times – toxic waste from the manufacture of Apple products, BP's Gulf of Mexico oil spill, Tesco & Findus's 'horseburgers' – were not caused directly by those big brands, but by their suppliers and contractors. You could say the supply chain is the Pandora's Box of the sustainability world. As Tom Smith of Sedex puts it, 'As you go down the supply chain, the sustainability risks are greater, you have less visibility, and you have less influence.'

Given the size of the task in tackling the supply chain, 80/20 thinking can help focus thinking down on the issues that matter.

Where are the impacts?

The most damaging industries in the economy tend to be in the primary sector: agriculture, forestry, fishing, mining and the extraction of oil and gas, along with the initial processing of those materials. For example, extracting 1 kg aluminium from bauxite ore in the ground produces 84 kg of waste (including 1–2 kg of toxic 'red mud'), requires 155 MJ of energy and releases perfluorocarbons (PFCs), powerful greenhouse gases. In contrast, recycling aluminium uses 5 percent of the energy required to extract virgin material and only produces 3 percent of the waste – a clear candidate for an 80/20 type solution.[22]

This means the 80/20 Rule can be applied vertically or horizontally to the supply chain. Horizontally, you identify the key first tier suppliers which present the biggest impacts/risk and address them as a priority. Vertically, the 80/20 Rule suggests that the most effective strategy is to eliminate those huge primary industry impacts by choosing low impact virgin materials (usually natural materials) or sourcing secondary (recycled) materials.

Standard practice

Unfortunately, supply chain sustainability is one area where bureaucracy has a tendency to strangle the very change it is meant to deliver. The ambition tends to be limited to encouraging suppliers to meet a minimum standard rather than to deliver a truly sustainable supply chain. There is also a tendency to cling to processes rather than focus on results. I was once asked during a Supply Chain Sustainability webinar how some of the powerful practical techniques I was describing would fit into the UK Government's 'Flexible Framework' on supply chain sustainability. It took a lot of self-control not to yell 'Who cares?!' at the questioner. The tail must not be allowed to wag the dog.

Supplier questionnaires

One of the key culprits in focusing supply chain sustainability management on process and incremental improvements is the ubiquitous supply chain questionnaire. Suppliers frequently complain that they spend more time translating the same information into different formats for different customers than actually doing something about the impacts. Tracey Rawling Church of Kyocera explains:

> *There is quite a lot of sustainable procurement window dressing going on out there. We are often asked to complete a very detailed questionnaire on our sustainability credentials – organisational carbon footprints, product carbon footprints, etc. That will get you on the shortlist but when it comes to actual bid, it's down to price. Every time we get asked this information, it is in a different format. Everybody's questionnaires are different.*

A number of supply chain reporting databases such as Sedex, Ecodesk and Ecovadis have sprung up to tackle this problem by allowing suppliers to provide the information once in a standard format and purchasers to access that information.

Minimum standards

Many organisations believe they are making a real difference by setting standards for their suppliers, for example, by requiring suppliers to hold ISO14001 or specifying paper from Forestry Stewardship Council (FSC) accredited sources. While such requirements are better than nothing, they merely lift the poorest performing suppliers up to an acceptable standard rather than creating the breakthrough changes required for sustainability.

80/20 thinking and the supply chain

In this section we will look at some of the supply chain techniques that will help us break away from the obsession with process and start making rapid change.

Creating an 'arms race'

The standard techniques discussed above depend on the purchaser to specify the environmental performance of a product or service. But clearly it is more effective to challenge your suppliers to go further and faster on their own volition.

Public sector organisations usually implement a formal scoring system for tenders with the available points typically split between criteria such as cost, performance, track record and risk. Many public bodies now allocate

10, 15 or even 30 percent of the total score to green and/or ethical issues – above and beyond any minimum standards. This means that, in a tight competition, a tenderer can win the contract by beating the opposition on green alone. This creates an 'arms race' between suppliers over time as each has to continuously improve their credentials to stay competitive. Glen Bennett of EAE Ltd says: 'In our tenders to Scottish public bodies, we find a picture of our wind turbine is worth 100 environmental policies.'

A similar approach can be taken with product specifications by requiring a minimum standard and reward those who exceed that standard, for example:

> *We require the vehicle to have carbon emissions of no more than 150 gCO_2/km. For every 10 g below this target we will award an extra 10 points.*[23]

Having ambitious sustainability targets can attract innovate suppliers keen to win business. InterfaceFLOR inspired a supplier, Aquafil, to start making yarn from old fishing nets pulled from the ocean. 'We continue to be impressed by what can be achieved when suppliers are encouraged to innovate and are rewarded for solving *our* problems instead of us trying to solve theirs,' says InterfaceFLOR's Ramon Arratia. 'We have witnessed how much more the "inspire, measure, innovate" approach can deliver than "code, questionnaire, audit".'

'My way or the highway'

More and more organisations are getting tough with recalcitrant suppliers – the stick to the carrot described above. Ramon Arratia of InterfaceFLOR puts it bluntly: 'Rather than ticking boxes and checking certificates and all that crap, if you stop doing business with a high impact supplier and start using low impact suppliers, things will start to change very quickly.' While many sustainability practitioners baulk at such brutal action, at the end of the day this is the only way to make change happen at pace.

Investing in the supply chain

So far we have assumed that the relationship between suppliers and purchasers is largely transactional. However, some cutting-edge businesses are going far beyond that traditional relationship and actively intervening in the supply chain (we'll be looking at the broader principle of Creating Shared Value in Chapter 8).

For example, Marks & Spencer went into collaboration with one of their lingerie suppliers in Sri Lanka to design and build an 'eco-factory' that requires only 4 percent of the energy of a traditional factory. The use of natural light and ventilation makes working conditions as far removed from the stereotype of the sweatshop as could be imagined.[24]

But other companies are going further and making investments which will benefit their suppliers. For example, Google is investing in developing renewable energy technologies, specifically the funding for projects which will make renewable power cheaper than coal power.[25] This investment is intended to develop future low carbon energy supplies both for Google itself and others, shaping future supply chains.

Paul Taylor of Camira explains why they have no problem with investments which could benefit competitors:

> *Many companies would wrestle with putting resource into getting suppliers organic certification or an EU eco-label, but it is our moral*

duty to make every metre of fabric as good as it can possibly be. At the end of the day it is growing our business and growing it on the principles of sustainability, so who cares if our competitors grow their business on the back of it too?

Building a new supply chain

As we saw above, one key 80/20 solution for the supply chain is to use recovered material. This ambition has been scaled up by the adoption of the 'circular economy' model where materials flow continuously in cycles, much the way carbon or water are cycled in nature.

But in practice such radical shifts suffer from the classic chicken-and-egg conundrum – until there is demand, there is no supply chain, but how can you create demand for something which doesn't exist? At the end of the day, demand is what will bring down prices and increase quality and security of supply, all key requirements of a mainstream sustainable supply chain. The 80/20 Rule then says focus on demand.

Marks & Spencer tackled the lack of a viable supply chain for high-grade recycled polyester for clothing by stimulating demand across their product range. They began purchasing large quantities of low-grade recycled fibre for bulk uses such as filling cushions. This demand stimulated the nascent supply chain and brought down the cost of high-grade recycled polyester fibre. Marks & Spencer hopes that the recycled fibre can soon be produced at a price that is competitive with virgin fibre.[26]

Another approach is Forward Commitment Procurement where buyers announce to suppliers in advance what the organisation would like out of a future product/service, how much it would want and by when. This de-risks the development of new product/services for suppliers, as they know there will be a market for that product/service if they get it right. For example, HM Prison Service set a forward commitment requirement in 2006 saying that by 2012 that they wanted to reduce their disposal of 40,000 polyurethane mattresses by 98 percent. The contract with the winning supplier was signed in 2009 and has been estimated to save HMPS £5 million over its duration.[27] By giving the suppliers several years to develop their ideas, confident in the knowledge that a contract would be let in the future, HMPS de-risked the innovation process.

Forward commitments can be made by partnerships to give an even bigger prize for suppliers willing to innovate. For example, in order to create sufficient demand for hydrogen-powered delivery vans, European postal services combined forces via the PostEurop organisation. By using forward commitment procurement and some hard bargaining, PostEurop believes it has brought forward the commercialisation of the technology by a decade. Again this shows the power that demand has on the market.[28]

Summary

As with employee engagement, supply chain sustainability is an area where far too many organisations are stuck at the 'trivial many' tasks which soak up a huge amount of resource while only delivering incremental improvements. Shifting to a truly sustainable supply chain requires a massive change, but using 80/20 techniques such as those described above, shifts the burden onto the supplier to innovate quickly to avoid losing custom – or to encourage new suppliers to disrupt the current market. While this is easier for organisations with large buying power, it benefits smaller outfits indirectly as the market shifts.

CHAPTER 7

Using the 80/20 Rule to Make Products and Services Sustainable

Overview

IT HAS BEEN SAID that design is the engine room of good environmental practice. Many sources say that 80 percent of product impacts are determined on the drawing board (e.g. the European Commission[29]). This mirrors the rule of thumb that 80 percent of life cycle costs are determined during design. Richard Koch goes even further, claiming that 20 percent of design time determines 80 percent of life cycle costs. In other words, relatively few decisions determine overall costs and, by extension, life cycle environmental impacts.

Using the Pareto analysis can have other benefits. In a study of drainage options, Jason King of landscape architects TERRA.fluxus found that trying to eliminate pipes altogether would triple the cost of the project compared to business as usual, but selecting the 80/20 solutions cut the cost of the project by 10 percent.[30] This suggests Pareto can help us get over 'paralysis by perfectionism' and find solutions which deliver environmental *and* economic benefits.

So eco-design is 80/20 thinking in itself, but there is still much that can be done to apply 80/20 thinking in the design process. If an 'eco-product' simply swaps one environmental problem for another – such as a cleaning product using unsustainable if natural palm oil instead of oil-derived chemicals – then sustainability improvements are going to be incremental at best. Many of the great examples below are driven by the mindset of the innovators to make breakthrough solutions, rather than incremental improvements.

80/20 rules of thumb

In the last chapter we saw that for most organisations, the bulk of the impacts 'cradle to gate' are deep in the supply chain. This applies for products which are relatively inert in use – a Coke can, for example. A typical solution here is to use secondary (recycled) materials in the place of virgin materials.

But for durable goods that consume energy and/or materials in their use phase such as vehicles, IT equipment, white goods or clothing, it is this phase that generally dominates life cycle footprint. So an energy efficient product such as a LED light bulb is a good example of how this can be addressed.

A third rule of thumb is to design persistent toxic chemicals out of the whole life cycle of the product. As eco-design gurus William McDonough and Michael Braungart say, 'we've got to take filters out of the pipes and put them where they belong, in the designers' heads'.[31]

With a little common sense, designers can use these simple 80/20 rules of thumb to make substantial improvements to the environmental performance of their products without the need for a detailed and costly Life Cycle Assessment (see Chapter 5).

80/20 thinking and eco-design

As studies have found that 80 percent of a car's carbon footprint is in the use phase, our rules of thumb from above indicate that designers need to focus on fuel efficiency as a priority.

Tesla's approach to electric vehicle has shaken up the industry. While other traditional car manufacturers have produced modest hatchbacks with limited range, Tesla first produced a sports car to attract attention, then a luxury sedan whose range of 300 miles makes it comparable to an internal combustion engine car.

Tesla also applies the kind of 80/20 thinking we saw in the supply chain (see Chapter 6) to its business model to bring volume to key components. Seeing the synergy with other energy markets, the company has been marketing its car batteries to homeowners to store renewable energy. The company has also announced its intention to allow its patented inventions to be used royalty-free by others. The thinking behind this is to maximise the volume of specialist electric vehicle components, bringing down costs for everyone which in turn means electric vehicles will command a bigger market share.[32]

The thinking big approach seems to be catching in the car world. Porsche has produced a hybrid supercar which can hit 210 mph, yet it emits less carbon than a Toyota Prius (under normal driving conditions, naturally).[33]

80/20 analysis and eco-design

That's not to say life cycle assessment isn't useful when resources permit. A great example is Ariel Excel Gel from Procter & Gamble. When P&G did an energy life cycle analysis of the typical clothes-washing product they

found that 75 percent of the energy was consumed in the use phase –
through the heating of water – and 10 percent was from the production
of raw materials. Everything else – manufacture, distribution, retail and
waste water treatment, etc. – added up to the final 15 percent.[34] This is
in line with the rules of thumb described above, but at the time, no-one
else had done a comparable study to confirm this.

Adopting an 80/20 approach to design, P&G developed Ariel Excel Gel
from scratch to tackle these two critical issues. The product will clean
clothes at near-cold water temperatures (15°C) and it is a compact to
minimise the amount of raw material used. They also designed it as a
product that mainstream consumers would actually use – award-winning
performance and a competitive price.

Rethinking problems into solutions

It's amazing what an innovative mindset can bring. JN Bentley Ltd was
commissioned to design a pump to maintain water levels over a canoe
course on the River Tees, pumping water back upstream during times
of low flow. While this might seem like a massive waste of energy to
many, the engineers threw the idea on its head. Using four reversible
Archimedes screws, the system generates clean hydroelectric electricity
when the river levels are high, then switches to pump the water upstream
if the course is needed during periods of low flow. This turned a problem
into a solution – from a questionable user of energy into a significant net
producer of clean energy, while letting the canoeists have their fun.[35]

Rethinking the product

A key 80/20 question is whether a product is required in the first place?
If not, then substantial environmental improvements can be made.

A product-service system is one where the idea of purchasing a product is replaced by leasing the product as part of a service. For example, under chemical management services, you purchase a solvent service instead of a barrel of solvent. The supplier will install and maintain any equipment, provide the solvent and remove the used solvent afterwards for recycling. Similarly, Xerox will sell you a photocopying service where it will provide, maintain and upgrade the copier and charge you per copy made. In both cases, it incentivises both supplier and purchaser to use/waste less material.

This move from products to services has been taken a stage further through digitisation where consumers now purchase substantial quantities of music, books, movies, news and photo services without ever handling a tangible product. This gives the consumer the service they want (a particular song) without any associated stuff (the CD, booklet, packaging) leading to substantial improvements in its ecological footprint. For example, it has been estimated that downloading an album of music has 20 percent of the carbon footprint of purchasing a CD (provided the downloader doesn't then burn the music to CD)[36] – and of course this residual carbon can be reduced further using renewable energy in data centres.

Summary

The design of products is another area where a huge amount of effort can be made for a negligible return on results if the focus is on detail rather than the big picture, that is, focusing on the 80 percent rather than the vital 20 percent. Far too many people end up substituting one environmental problem for another, but this can largely be avoided by focusing on the 20 percent of variables that matter and applying common sense to avoid displacing problems instead of designing them out.

Here are the key 80/20 questions in eco-design, the answers to which will deliver the vast bulk of potential improvements:

- Is a product necessary? What is the function of the product and can it be delivered under a completely different business model?

- Can we deliver a product that turns an environmental problem into a solution?

- How can we radically reduce the materials required?

- How can we make this product part of the circular economy (recycled material in a product designed for recycling)?

- How can we radically improve the energy efficiency of the product in use (if appropriate)?

- How can we phase out all persistent toxic materials throughout the life cycle?

- Is the product/service attractive to the market (aesthetics, price, quality)?

Of course design is not quite as simple as this and common sense needs to be applied to avoid unintended consequences, but it follows that 80 percent of the design effort should be aimed at tackling these vital ssues.

....

CHAPTER 8

80/20 and Strategy

IN THE PREVIOUS CHAPTERS we have looked at applications of the 80/20 Rule to specific elements of corporate sustainability. In this chapter we will look at strategic approaches to embed 80/20 thinking on sustainability into the organisation. Here are five strategies (in ascending order of ambition).

Optimum number of targets

In an article to my mailing list, The Low Carbon Agenda, I recently recommended that the maximum number of sustainability targets an organisation should adopt was seven. An adherent of 'One Planet Living' challenged that statement as the OPL system has 10 Principles.[37] My arguments for fewer targets are:

- Seven is regarded as the longest list that most people can remember without having to make an effort. This is known as Miller's Law after the psychologist who discovered the phenomenon (strictly speaking Miller's 'magic number' is 7±2).[38]

- If you have too many targets and you can justify a sub-optimal solution by saying 'well, it meets targets 3, 4, 6, 7 and 9. . .' when the major issue is target 1.

- The 80/20 Rule says focus on what matters – having a smaller set of targets gives you that focus.

To take a prominent example, retail giant WalMart has set just three overarching targets:[39]

- Energy: be supplied 100% by renewable energy.

- Waste: create zero waste.

- Products: sell products that sustain people and the environment.

Of course these top-level targets are supported by a large number of subsidiary goals, but it is a boon to have such a simple, clear declaration of intent that people can rally around. It also encourages 80/20 thinking by focusing on what matters.

Stretch targets

Many organisations set incremental targets for sustainability, such as 'we will reduce our carbon footprint by 2 percent year on year'. This focuses effort and attention on the 20 percent of 'quick wins' rather than the 80 percent of the impact. After a couple of years, when most of the 'low hanging fruit' have been picked, this becomes a mad hunt for more incremental improvement. Such organisations end up on the 'diminishing returns' trajectory of the sloping staircase model.

Roberta Barbieri of Diageo told me of her company's Damascene conversion to stretch targets:

The big change occurred a few years ago when we decided that, instead of trying to get incremental improvements in our performance, we would take the leap to make step change improvements.

This small change in strategy – moving from incremental targets to a stretch target of 50 percent reduction in carbon emissions by 2015 – led to the construction of several anaerobic digestion plants at Diageo's distilleries to turn wastewater into clean energy. At the time, these were the biggest renewable energy projects in the UK outside the energy sector. By setting stretch targets, the company had to focus on the vital 20 percent of issues which determine its impact and drop its hunt for quick wins which usually sit in the other 80 percent.

Sustainability by innovation

The stretch target approach above is still 'sustainability by target' where you set a target and work out how to hit it. But many businesses are going beyond this by using metrics to identify their biggest impacts and then relentlessly tackling those hotspots head on. I call this 'sustainability by innovation'.

A great example is Procter & Gamble's Ariel Excel Gel. As we saw in Chapter 7, a life cycle assessment of clothes-washing products showed that 75 percent of their carbon footprint arose from heating water in the washing machine. So P&G developed Ariel Excel Gel to wash clothes at 15°C to slash that impact.

Such innovation is unlikely to be delivered to meet a target – it takes a much more proactive mindset to seek out and tackle problems in this way. In fact, metrics may have to temporarily take a back seat. As Paul Taylor, Sustainability Manager of Camira Fabrics puts it:

Sustainability by innovation means always saying 'that's not enough'. Your metrics may slip away a bit while you innovate, but your ambition is to go miles beyond what you would ever be driven to by a metric.

This need for a restless mindset is echoed by Muhtar Kent, Chairman of the Board and CEO of Coca-Cola:

Sustainability is an on-going journey, one that we hope and trust will build forward momentum as we remain 'constructively discontent'. . . recognizing achievement but also understanding that we can never be satisfied with it. We must refuse to accept the status quo and continue to challenge ourselves.[40]

Sustainability as the core business strategy

A further step beyond the 'sustainability by innovation' approach is to hitch the future of the business to the sustainability bandwagon.

For example, Camira Fabrics sees sustainability as the engine of growth in the business, using it to find business opportunities to exploit. My favourite example is when the company took used coffee sacks from Starbucks and blended the fibres into a fabric for seats in Starbucks stores, creating a product with a great story behind it. As Sustainability Manager Paul Taylor puts it:

We are committed to building a sustainable value chain and that leads to growth, that's an income generator, that's profitable. Our turnover was £26m in 2006, now [2013] it's £70m. And that's been purely from a drive for sustainability.

Jeff Immelt, Chairman and CEO of General Electric puts it like this: 'Sustainability is our business strategy. It's our roadmap for how we operate & innovate.' The prime mover of this strategy at GE has been the Ecomagination programme set up to identify and develop business opportunities in green technology. The company claims that, by early 2014, Ecomagination had generated more than $160 billion in revenue. GE's own operations have seen a 34 percent reduction in greenhouse gas emissions since 2004 and a 47 percent reduction in freshwater use since 2006, realising $300 million in savings. In 2014, the company announced a further $10 billion in the period 2015–2020 taking the overall investment to $25 billion.[41]

There are many other great examples. The corporate purpose of BASF is: 'We create chemistry for a sustainable future.' This places sustainability front and centre of the business's whole reason for existing. One of my clients, Johnson Matthey plc, estimates that over 80 percent of their turnover comes from products that protect the environment such as catalytic convertors for cars and industrial pollution prevention systems. In an interesting twist, this means the tighter regulations become, the more profit they make.

Obviously such a strategy is high risk as it involves innovative business models and developing new supply chains. But companies such as Johnson Matthey, Camira and GE show it can be done.

Creating Shared Value (CSV)

The Creating Shared Value (CSV) concept emerged in 2011, the brainchild of business gurus Michael Porter and Mark Kramer. They believe that Corporate Social Responsibility (CSR) is too narrow in scope to bring step improvements to social and environmental issues in the economy. It involves actively investing in the business eco-system around your organisation for the benefit of all.[42] The classic example is Nike's promotion of active lifestyles. Society benefits from better public health, and the market for sportswear grows which in turn benefits Nike – and their competitors. In many ways, CSV is the epitome of the 'abundance mentality' – that there is plenty of value for everyone.

We have already discussed several examples of CSV-style thinking in Chapters 6 and 7:

- Camira's work to improve the whole wool supply chain.

- Tesla's opening up of their patented technologies to others, to create demand and volume for electric vehicle components.

- Google's investment in renewable energy technology.

All of these examples will benefit competitors as well as the company itself. However, the company's involved see the benefits outweighing any potential commercial. This ambitious thinking allows business to unlock 80/20 type solutions by removing perceived barriers to progress.

Summary

In summary, to use the 80/20 Rule, it needs to be embedded deep into the organisation's strategy. As we have seen in the sections above, the following steps will achieve this:

- A relatively small number of ambitious stretch targets.

- A restless innovation mindset, never satisfied with progress, but always wanting to do more.

- The alignment of the core business purpose to the business.

- A broad vision of sustainability where external investment is made for the benefit of all.

....

CHAPTER 9

Conclusions

YOU WILL GATHER BY NOW that a huge frustration of mine is that a high proportion of what sustainability practitioners do is activity for activity's sake. We get networks of green champions, 'engagement' which focuses on employees' personal lives instead of their day job and endless supplier questionnaires. At best, this is done because that's what other sustainability practitioners do; at worst, it is deliberately avoiding the elephant in the room.

One key benefit of the 80/20 Rule is that by forcing you to concentrate on the 80 percent of your impacts rather than the trivial 20 percent, you tackle sustainability elephants head on, avoiding 'greenwash' if nothing else. If you treat all problems as equal, then you can end up wasting energy on cracking insignificant but difficult problems when more significant problems may actually be easier to solve.

Even if those problems are difficult, by 'zooming in' on a core set of objectives, the efforts, experience and ingenuity of your colleagues get focused on the issues that matter, rather than trying to 'do everything'. Too many sustainability efforts deliberately try to catch every issue in a big net, confusing and intimidating colleagues, and ultimately leading to overwhelm.

The 80/20 approach can help with two other causes of organisational paralysis:

- Paralysis by analysis where the pursuit of data and 'facts' becomes more important than acting on them.

- Paralysis by perfection where the solutions proposed are never good enough (some environmental activists have made a career out of intoning 'that's no good because . . .' without ever proposing a solution which does meet their exemplary standards).

80/20 overcomes this paralysis, by saying 'forget the detail, once we see the broad way forward, let's get going and learn as we move forward'. It is really rather liberating and rewarding from a personal point of view.

The 80/20 Rule can be seen as rather brutal, or even Darwinian, but I sometimes worry that sustainability practitioners are too nice. We are driven by the desire to make the world a better place and our instincts are harmonious rather than hard-headed. So we end up like one of those old-fashioned plate-spinning variety acts, dashing around trying to keep dozens of plates from falling to the floor. But tackling existential global challenges such as climate change, resource depletion or biodiversity loss won't be solved by niceties alone. We need to separate the wheat from the chaff, focus on the issues that really matter, and then focus on the solutions to those issues that will have the biggest impact and pursue those relentlessly.

The time for beating around the bush has gone, and the 80/20 Rule gives us the mindset to make a real difference to the future of our society and the planet it depends on. Let's do it!

Notes and References

1. Confino, J. 2013. The conundrum at the heart of sustainability. *The Guardian*, http://www.theguardian.com/sustainable-business/conundrum-heart-sustainability

2. Profile taken from *Encyclopaedia Britannica*, http://www.britannica.com/EBchecked/topic/443519/Vilfredo-Pareto

3. Profile taken from *Encyclopaedia Britannica*, http://www.britannica.com/EBchecked/topic/1314830/Joseph-Moses-Juran

4. Koch, R. 1998. *The 80/20 Principle* (London: Nicholas Brealey).

5. Ibid.

6. Ferriss, T. 2007. *The Four Hour Work Week* (London: Vermillion).

7. Ortiz, I. and Cummins, M. 2011. Global inequality: Beyond the bottom billion. UNICEF, http://www.unicef.org/socialpolicy/files/Global_Inequality.pdf

8. Podobnik, B. 2002. Global energy inequalities: Exploring the long-term implications. *Journal of World-Systems Research* (Volume viii, Issue 2): 252–274.

9. Lawrence, S., Liu, Q. and Yakovenko, V.M., 2013. Global inequality in energy consumption from 1980 to 2010. *Entropy* (Vol. 15): 5565–5579.

10. Wild, S. 2013. How to be green – Pareto guide to sustainability, http://simonwild.me/2013/07/29/how-to-be-green-pareto-guide-to-sustainability/

11. Institute of Mechanical Engineers, 2011. Life cycle assessment: Road vehicle emissions measurement, http://www.imeche.org/docs/default-source/position-statements-transport/IMechE_Life_Cycle_PS.pdf

12. Personal communication, H. Park, BBC Sustainability Manager, 3 November 2011.

13. Life Cycle Inventory on laundry detergents: An analysis of LCI profiles of liquids and powder detergents, http://www.abnt.org.br/cb38/Arquivos/Lyfe%20 Cycle.pdf

14. Energy Saving Trust, 2011. Lit up: an LED lighting field trial, http://www. energysavingtrust.org.uk/Publications2/Energy-efficiency/Lit-up-an-LED-lighting-field-trial

15. Anderson, R. 2009. *Confessions of a Radical Industrialist* (London: Random House).

16. 2degrees, 2014. Overcoming the engagement barrier: 2degrees sustainable business trends tracker, https://www.2degreesnetwork.com/ groups/2degrees-community/resources/engagement-biggest-challenge-driving-sustainable-business/

17. Kane, G. 2012. *Green Jujitsu: The Smart Way to Embed Sustainability in Your Organisation* (Oxford: DōSustainability).

18. Kane, G. 2011. *The Green Executive* (London: Earthscan).

19. Anderson, R. 2009. *Confessions of a Radical Industrialist* (London: Random House).

20. GRI, 2013. G4 Sustainability Reporting Guidelines.

21. Data taken from 'Canon Sustainability Report 2009', www.canon.com/ environment/report/pdf/report2009e.pdf, 'NHS England carbon footprint: GHG emissions, 1990–2020 baseline emissions update', National Health Service Sustainable Development Unit, www.sdu.nhs.uk/page.php?page_ id=160, Unilever Sustainable Living Plan, http://www.unilever.com/images/ UnileverSustainableLivingPlan_tcm13-284876.pdf and Apple and the Environment, http://www.apple.com/uk/environment/our-footprint/

22. The data in this section are sourced from The Minerals, Metals & Materials Society (TMS), http://www.tms.org/pubs/Books/4062.chapter2.pdf, Circular Ecology, http://www.circularecology.com/embodied-energy-and-carbon-

footprint-database.html#.VCWCHksac9U and the Global Development Research Centre, http://www.gdrc.org/uem/footprints/rucksacks.html

23. Example taken from BS903:2010 Principles and Framework for Procuring Sustainably, British Standards Institute.

24. Kane, G. 2011. *The Green Executive* (London: Earthscan).

25. Google.org, www.google.org/rec.html

26. Kane, G. 2011. *The Green Executive* (London: Earthscan).

27. FCP Demonstration Project: HM Prison Service Zero Waste Prison Mattress System, http://www.sustainable-procurement.org/fileadmin/template/scripts/sp_resources/_tools/put_file.php?uid=8dba396b

28. Kane, G. 2011. *The Green Executive* (London: Earthscan).

29. http://ec.europa.eu/energy/efficiency/ecodesign/eco_design_en.htm

30. http://landscapeandurbanism.blogspot.co.uk/2008/05/8020-for-sustainability.html

31. McDonough, W. and Braungart, M. 2003. *Cradle to Cradle: Remaking the Way We Make Things* (New York: Rodale Press).

32. Decker, S., Ohnsman, A. and Clothier, M. 2014. Musk applies contrarian style to patents to boost Tesla. *Bloomberg*, 13 June.

33. *BBC Top Gear*, 2013. Porsche 918: The ultimate verdict, http://www.topgear.com/uk/car-news/porsche-918-spyder-first-drive-2013-11-26

34. Life cycle inventory on laundry detergents: An analysis of LCI profiles of liquids and powder detergents, http://www.abnt.org.br/cb38/Arquivos/Lyfe%20Cycle.pdf

35. http://www.waterprojectsonline.com/case_studies/2011/Hydropower_Tees_%20Whitewater_2011.pdf

36. Weber, C.L., Koomey, J.G. and Matthews, H.S., 2009. The energy and climate

change impacts of different music delivery methods, http://download.intel.com/pressroom/pdf/CDsvsdownloadsrelease.pdf

37. One Planet Living website, http://www.oneplanetliving.net/what-is-one-planet-living/the-ten-principles/

38. Miller, G.A. 1956. The magical number seven, plus or minus two: Some limits on our capacity for processing information. *Psychological Review* (Volume 63): 81–97.

39. Walmart website sustainability pages, http://corporate.walmart.com/global-responsibility/environmental-sustainability

40. Gallo, A. 2014. The CEO of Coca-Cola on using the company's scale for good. *Harvard Business Review Blog,* http://blogs.hbr.org/2014/05/the-ceo-of-coca-cola-on-using-the-companys-scale-for-good/

41. General Electric News Centre, 2014. GE renews ecomagination commitments, http://www.genewscenter.com/Press-Releases/GE-Renews-Ecomagination-Commitments-454d.aspx

42. Porter, M. and Kramer, M. 2011. Creating shared value. *Harvard Business Review* (Volume 89, Issue 1/2): 62–77.

....

For Product Safety Concerns and Information please contact our EU
representative GPSR@taylorandfrancis.com
Taylor & Francis Verlag GmbH, Kaufingerstraße 24, 80331 München, Germany

www.ingramcontent.com/pod-product-compliance
Ingram Content Group UK Ltd.
Pitfield, Milton Keynes, MK11 3LW, UK
UKHW040928180425
457613UK00011B/287